FITTING WORDS

Workbook

FITTING WORDS

CLASSICAL RHETORIC

Workbook

ROMAN ROADS
MEDIA

In this series:

Resource
Fitting Words Textbook
Fitting Words Student Workbook (this book)
Fitting Words Answer Key
Fitting Words Exam Pack
Fitting Words Video Course

Fitting Words Student Workbook
Second Edition (Version 2.0.0)

Copyright © 2018 by Roman Roads Media, LLC
Copyright © 2016 by Roman Roads Media, LLC

Published by Roman Roads Media
Moscow, Idaho
www.romanroadsmedia.com

Cover design by Rachel Rosales (Orange Peal Design).
Interior illustration by George Harrell. Interior design by Valerie Anne Bost.

Unless otherwise indicated, Scripture quotations are from the New King James Version of the Bible, ©1979, 1980, 1982, 1984, 1988 by Thomas Nelson, Inc., Nashville, Tennessee.

All rights reserved. No part of this publication may be reproduced, stored in a retrieval system, or transmitted in any form by any means, electronic, mechanical, photocopy, recording, or otherwise, without prior permission of the publisher, except as provided by USA copyright law.

ISBN-13: 978-1-944482-30-5
ISBN-10: 1-944482-30-X

TABLE OF CONTENTS

Components of This Course vii
Optional Course Schedules. ix

LESSON EXERCISES

Exercise 1 1	Exercise 15a 51	Exercise 23a 105
Exercise 2 3	Exercise 15b 55	Exercise 23b 109
Exercise 3 5	Exercise 16a 57	Exercise 24a 115
Exercise 4 9	Exercise 16b 63	Exercise 24b 117
Exercise 5 13	Exercise 17a 69	Exercise 25a 121
Exercise 6 17	Exercise 17b 71	Exercise 25b 125
Exercise 7 21	Exercise 18a 75	Exercise 26a 127
Exercise 8 23	Exercise 18b 77	Exercise 26b 131
Exercise 9 25	Exercise 19a 81	Exercise 27a 135
Exercise 10 27	Exercise 19b 83	Exercise 27b 141
Exercise 11 31	Exercise 20 87	Exercise 28a 145
Exercise 12 35	Exercise 21a 91	Exercise 28b 149
Exercise 13 39	Exercise 21b 95	Exercise 29 153
Exercise 14a 43	Exercise 22a 97	Exercise 30a 155
Exercise 14b 47	Exercise 22b 101	Exercise 30b 161

Works Cited in Exercises. 163
Speech Judging Sheets 165

COMPONENTS OF THIS COURSE

Fitting Words: Classical Rhetoric for the Christian Student is meant as a one-year course in practical rhetoric for the Christian high school student. The entire packet includes these components:

1. The **textbook** with thirty lessons on the art of rhetoric. Each lesson also includes Thinking Deeper questions, suggestions for Reading Further, and quotes for Developing Memory. The Thinking Deeper sections provide optional questions for discussion, questions which dig further into the lesson topics. These occasionally require outside reading. The Developing Memory sections give the students exercise in memorizing and delivering appropriate quotes of varying length. Before starting this course you may find it helpful to read Lesson 29, which discusses some methods for memorizing. Students will write and deliver speeches after Lessons 13, 14, 15, 16, and 30. The appendices include a glossary of key terms, the text of the primary speeches used throughout the course, and a chart of every speech in the Bible, many of which are also used throughout the course.

2. The **student workbook**, which includes exercises for each lesson. Many of the lessons have two exercises, A and B, both of which should be completed by the student before going on to the next lesson. Also included are speech judging sheets identical to those in the test packet, which the student may use to evaluate himself as he practices the required speeches.

3. An **answer key** for the exercises and the tests. Also included is a proposed course schedule. The answer key layout matches the layout of the exercises and tests for ease of grading. Point suggestions are given [in brackets] for the exams only.

4. The **exam packet**, which includes review sheets for the tests, the tests themselves, and speech judging sheets for the instructor to evaluate the speeches to be delivered by the student. The final evaluation for the course is not a comprehensive exam but a final speech. Review sheets, tests, and judging

sheets are items which may be individually copied and distributed to the students at various times throughout the course.

5. In the **video course** that accompanies this text, each lesson is introduced and taught through two videos: a main lesson video which walks you through the lesson from the textbook, and a seperate application video which walks students through the exercises. Each lesson also introduces a figure of speech or thought (retaught together in Lessons 27 and 28), and suggestions for the optional Thinking Deeper discussions. The video also includes 9 exam prep videos.

HOW TO USE THIS WORKBOOK

This student workbook includes the lesson exercises and speech judging sheets for *Fitting Words: Classical Rhetoric*. This workbook is consumable; each student should be issued one workbook. The exercise numbers are aligned with the lesson numbers in the student text. The answers for these exercises are contained in the Answer Key for *Fitting Words*.

Speech judging sheets are included here for the students to use as they practice their speeches. Identical speech judging sheets are included in the test packet for instructor use.

EXERCISE 1

NAME

DATE

1. Name and explain three distinct things a speaker can do to make his speech *in*effective. Find three passages not referenced in the lesson where the Bible speaks about how we should speak: one from Proverbs, one from Jesus in the Gospels, and a third from elsewhere in the New Testament. Draw one practical application for rhetoric from each.

2. Find three passages not referenced in the lesson where the Bible speaks about how we should speak: one from Proverbs, one from Jesus in the gospels, and a third from elsewhere in the New Testament. Draw one practical application for rhetoric from each.

EXERCISE 2

NAME

DATE

Consider this structural analysis of an excerpt from Gorgias's *Encomium of Helen*. Note that parallel (meaning similar or opposite) words or phrases are placed one above the other.

> In many did she work desire for her love, and
> her one body was the cause of bringing together
>   many bodies of men
>   thinking great thoughts for
>   great goals,
>   of whom some had greatness of wealth,
>   some the glory of ancient nobility,
>   some the vigor of personal agility,
>   some the command of acquired knowledge.
> And all came because of a passion which loved to conquer and
>   a love of honor which was unconquered.

Arrange the following brief speeches from the Old Testament using this same method.

1. Ruth 1:16–17

2. 1 Samuel 17:45–47

EXERCISE 3

NAME

DATE

1. What is the first thing that Socrates says a good speaker must know? Contrary to this, what has Phaedrus heard to be the source of persuasion for orators? [259–260]

2. What does Lady Rhetoric claim that she is able to give? What does she not claim to give?

3. Phaedrus says that the practice of rhetoric has been confined to courts of law and public assemblies. In the lines prior, what does Socrates imply that its scope should be? [261]

4. What does Socrates criticize the professors of the art of rhetoric (he has in mind the sophists) for doing?

5. Socrates claims that "he who would be a master of the art must understand the real nature of everything." Explain why (there are a couple of reasons). [262]

6. Having listened to the first few lines of Lysias's speech, what two suggestions does Socrates make for the rhetorician (what ought he to do, and what must he observe)? What does he further imply that a rhetorician should do (that Lysias did not do)? [263]

Fitting Words: Workbook | EXERCISE 3

7. Having heard the first few lines of Lysias's speech for a second time, what further suggestion does Socrates make regarding the practice of rhetoric? [264]

8. What additional two principles must rhetoricians follow, according to Socrates? [265–266]

EXERCISE 4

NAME

DATE

1. List in order the parts of a discourse noted by Socrates (there are about eight of them) that were to be found in the handbooks of rhetoric. [266–267]

2. Socrates makes an analogy between the rhetoricians of his day and those who would misuse the arts of medicine, tragedy, and music. Explain the analogy, and summarize his related criticism of rhetoric. [268–269, 272]

3. According to Socrates, what the three things must one have to be "a distinguished speaker"? [269]

4. What must a true rhetorician know about the soul? Explain what this means. [271–272]

5. Summarize the method of basing argument on probability. How does this method go astray, according to Socrates? [272–273]

6. Socrates summarizes his suggestions for developing rhetoric as a true art. Rewrite three of these suggestions in a brief, coherent paragraph. [273–274, 277]

EXERCISE 5

NAME

DATE

1. Write a thesis statement on a topic that interests you. Make sure that your statement is disputable, provable, clear, and interesting. This statement will be used in later exercises, as well.

2. For the thesis statement above, develop specific questions of stasis. Include at least two specific questions for each of the four categories. Then briefly answer the questions.

   Conjecture: _____

Definition: _____

_____
_____
_____
_____
_____
_____
_____
_____
_____
_____
_____
_____

Quality: _____

_____
_____
_____
_____
_____
_____
_____
_____
_____
_____
_____
_____
_____
_____

Policy: _____

EXERCISE 6

NAME

DATE

1. Consider your thesis statement and answers to Exercise 5. Write a brief introduction for a speech on your topic from the first six types of introduction presented in this lesson, and identify which type(s) you use. You may invent a fictitious setting for the speech.

_____
_____
_____
_____
_____
_____
_____
_____
_____
_____
_____
_____
_____
_____
_____
_____
_____

2. Read this introduction of *Here I Stand*, in which Martin Luther defends himself before the Diet of Worms (an imperial deliberative body held in Worms, Germany, in 1521).

> Most Serene Emperor, and you illustrious princes and gracious lords: I this day appear before you in all humility, according to your command, and I implore Your Majesty and your august highnesses, by the mercies of God, to listen with favor to the defense of a cause which I am well assured is just

17

and right. I ask pardon, if by reason of my ignorance, I am wanting in the manners that befit a court; for I have not been brought up in kings' palaces, but in the seclusion of a cloister.

This introduction primarily refers to the occasion of the speech. Rewrite it with Luther asking questions, instead, including in them most of the same information.

_____
_____
_____
_____
_____
_____
_____
_____
_____
_____
_____
_____

3. Read the introduction to Cicero's *First Oration Against Catiline*, delivered before the Roman Senate in 63 BC.

When, O Catiline, do you mean to cease abusing our patience? How long is that madness of yours still to mock us? When is there to be an end of that unbridled audacity of yours, swaggering about as it does now? Do not the nightly guards placed on the Palatine Hill—do not the watches posted throughout the city—does not the alarm of the people, and the union of all good men—does not the precaution taken of assembling the senate in this most defensible place—do not the looks and countenances of this venerable body here present, have any effect upon you? Do you not feel that your plans are detected? Do you not see that your conspiracy is already arrested and rendered powerless by the knowledge which every one here possesses of it? What is there that you did last night, what the night before—where

Fitting Words: Workbook | EXERCISE 6   **19**

is it that you were—who was there that you summoned to meet you—what design was there which was adopted by you, with which you think that any one of us is unacquainted?

This introduction directs rhetorical questions to the conspirator Catiline himself. Rewrite it by turning the questions into statements directed to the Senate. Include in it most of the same information.

_____
_____
_____
_____
_____
_____
_____
_____
_____
_____
_____
_____
_____
_____
_____
_____
_____
_____
_____
_____
_____
_____

4. Consider your rewritten introductions from the previous two questions. How do the revised introductions affect the tone of each speech?

EXERCISE 7

NAME

DATE

1. Consider Stephen's speech in Acts 7:2–53. Which verses constitute the narration? Defend your answer.

2. Considering the thesis statement and questions of stasis from Exercise 5, along with the introduction from Exercise 6, write a division for a speech on that topic. Include the points of agreement and contention, and a preview of the arguments.

EXERCISE 8

NAME

DATE

1. Read Acts 17:22–31. Most of Paul's speech (after verse 23) consists of proof. His thesis is in the second part of verse 29. Summarize four arguments of his proof, each written as an enthymeme (a statement with a supporting premise). Include verse numbers.

2. In the first two chapters of Romans, Paul argues that Jews and Gentiles are both alike under sin. Then in chapter three he presents a refutation section. Write out the first four objections—written as rhetorical questions—from Romans 3:1–9. (Note that some of the objections include two distinct questions, so the answer will comprise more than four questions.) Include the verse numbers.

EXERCISE 9

NAME

DATE

1. Woodrow Wilson's April 2, 1917, war speech, famous for declaring, "The world must be made safe for democracy," concludes with these two sentences:

   > To such a task we can dedicate our lives and our fortunes, everything that we are and everything that we have, with the pride of those who know that the day has come when America is privileged to spend her blood and her might for the principles that gave her birth and happiness and the peace which she has treasured. God helping her, she can do no other.

   Wilson here alludes to conclusions from two other famous speeches (both of which are included in Appendix A). Name them, and put the quotes from the originals next to the phrases from this conclusion for comparison.

Problems 2–10: Identify the type of conclusion used in each of these biblical speeches. The verses that make up the conclusion are identified in parentheses. (Hint: Each type is used at least once, none more than twice.)

2. Genesis 13:8–9 (9b) _____

3. Genesis 44:18–34 (33–34) _____

4. Exodus 13:3–16 (16) _____

5. Deuteronomy 29:2—30:20 (30:19–20) _____

6. Joshua 1:16–18 (18b) _____

7. 1 Kings 18:9–14 (14) _____

8. 1 Chronicles 22:7–16 (16b) _____

9. Matthew 10:5–42 (41–42) _____

10. Acts 20:18–35 (35b) _____

EXERCISE 10

NAME

DATE

1. Which elements of ethos are mentioned by Christ when he sends out the twelve to preach (Matt. 10:16)? Explain your answer.

2. Read the introduction to Martin Luther's *Here I Stand* speech before the Diet of Worms. How does Luther establish each of the three parts of ethos? Defend your answers.

> Most Serene Emperor, and you illustrious princes and gracious lords: I this day appear before you in all humility, according to your command, and I implore Your Majesty and your august highnesses, by the mercies of God, to listen with favor to the defense of a cause which I am well assured is just and right. I ask pardon, if by reason of my ignorance, I am wanting in the manners that befit a court; for I have not been brought up in kings' palaces, but in the seclusion of a cloister.

3. Read the excerpt from Letter from a Birmingham Jail. Where does Martin Luther King Jr. establish each of the three parts of ethos? Defend your answers.

> My Dear Fellow Clergymen:
> While confined here in the Birmingham city jail, I came across your recent statement calling my present activities "unwise and untimely." Seldom do I pause to answer criticism of my work and ideas. If I sought to answer all the criticisms that cross my desk, my secretaries would have little time for anything other than such correspondence in the course of the day, and I would have no time for constructive work. But since I feel that you are men of genuine good will and that your criticisms are sincerely set forth, I want to try to answer your statement in what I hope will be patient and reasonable terms.
> I think I should indicate why I am here in Birmingham, since you have been influenced by the view which argues against "outsiders coming in." I have the honor of serving as president of the Southern Christian Leadership Conference, an organization operating in every southern state, with headquarters in Atlanta, Georgia. We have some eighty five affiliated organizations across the South, and one of them is the Alabama Christian Movement for Human Rights. Frequently we share staff, educational and financial resources with our affiliates. Several months ago the affiliate here in Birmingham asked us to be on call to engage in a nonviolent direct action program if such were deemed necessary. We readily consented, and when the hour came we lived up to our promise. So I, along with several members of my staff, am here because I was invited here. I am here because I have organizational ties here.
> But more basically, I am in Birmingham because injustice is here. Just as the prophets of the eighth century B.C. left their villages and carried their "thus saith the Lord" far beyond the boundaries of their home towns, and just as the Apostle Paul left his village of Tarsus and carried the gospel of Jesus Christ to the far corners of the Greco Roman world, so am I compelled to carry the gospel of freedom beyond my own home town. Like Paul, I must constantly respond to the Macedonian call for aid.
> Moreover, I am cognizant of the interrelatedness of all communities and states. I cannot sit idly by in Atlanta and not be concerned about what happens in Birmingham. Injustice anywhere is a threat to justice everywhere. We are caught in an inescapable network of mutuality, tied in a single garment of destiny.

EXERCISE 11

NAME _____

DATE _____

Problems 1–5: One indication that it is proper to appeal to emotions is the fact that the Bible often speaks of men whose hearts are hardened against feeling appropriate emotions. Look up the given verses and identify the emotion that hearts are hardened against. (It may help you to read the definitions of the various emotion in Lessons 12 and 13.)

1. Exodus 9:11–12 _____
2. Deuteronomy 2:26–30 _____
3. Deuteronomy 15:7 _____
4. Proverbs 28:14 _____
5. Isaiah 63:17 _____

Problems 6–8: Read the refutation and conclusion of Patrick Henry's "Give Me Liberty" speech, and answer the related questions. (Line numbers have been added for convenience.)

¹They tell us, sir, that we are weak—unable to cope with so formidable an adversary. ²But when shall we be stronger? ³Will it be the next week, or the next year? ⁴Will it be when we are totally disarmed, and when a British guard shall be stationed in every house? ⁵Shall we gather strength by irresolution and inaction? ⁶Shall we acquire the means of effectual resistance by lying supinely on our backs and hugging the delusive phantom of hope, until our enemies shall have bound us hand and foot?

⁷Sir, we are not weak if we make a proper use of those means which the God of nature hath placed in our power. ⁸Three millions of people, armed in the holy cause of liberty, and in such a country as that which we possess, are invincible by any force which our enemy can send against us. ⁹Besides, sir, we shall not fight our battles alone. ¹⁰There is a just God who presides over the destinies of nations, and who will raise up friends to fight our battles for us. ¹¹The battle, sir, is not to the strong alone; it is to the vigilant, the active, the brave. ¹²Besides, sir, we have no election. ¹³If we were base enough to desire it, it is now too late to retire from the contest. ¹⁴There is

no retreat but in submission and slavery! ¹⁵Our chains are forged! ¹⁶Their clanking may be heard on the plains of Boston! ¹⁷The war is inevitable—and let it come! ¹⁸I repeat it, sir, let it come!

¹⁹It is in vain, sir, to extenuate the matter. ²⁰Gentlemen may cry, Peace, Peace—but there is no peace. ²¹The war is actually begun! ²²The next gale that sweeps from the north will bring to our ears the clash of resounding arms! ²³Our brethren are already in the field! ²⁴Why stand we here idle? ²⁵What is it that gentlemen wish? ²⁶What would they have? ²⁷Is life so dear, or peace so sweet, as to be purchased at the price of chains and slavery? ²⁸Forbid it, Almighty God! ²⁹I know not what course others may take; but as for me, give me liberty or give me death!

6. Describe the emotional impact of the rhetorical questions in the first and third paragraphs (lines 2–6 and 24–27). What emotion was Henry seeking to produce in his opponents (who opposed mobilizing for war)?

_____

_____

_____

_____

_____

7. The rhetorical question in line 6 uses *enargia* to create a clear image in the minds of the audience. Rewrite it an as ordinary declarative sentence with no figurative language. How does this change affect the emotional impact?

_____

_____

_____

_____

_____

_____

_____

8. What emotion is he seeking to produce in the middle paragraph, especially lines 7–11? How do lines 17–18 and line 29 help to reinforce that emotion?

EXERCISE 12

NAME _____

DATE _____

Problems 1–12: Identify the primary emotion from each lesson (anger, calmness, friendship, enmity, fear, confidence) that the given speaker is seeking to produce in his hearers.

1. Genesis 13:8–9 _____
2. Exodus 14:13–14 _____
3. Joshua 22:22–29 _____
4. 1 Samuel 25:24–31 _____
5. 1 Kings 1:17–21, 24–27 _____
6. 1 Kings 5:2–9 _____
7. 2 Chronicles 13:4–7 _____
8. Ezra 6:6–12 _____
9. Daniel 3:9–12 _____
10. Matthew 28:18–20 _____
11. Mark 9:42–48 _____
12. Acts 24:5–8 _____

13. Which emotion is Martin Luther trying to produce in the introduction to *Here I Stand?* Defend your answer.

    Most Serene Emperor, and you illustrious princes and gracious lords: I this day appear before you in all humility, according to your command, and I implore Your Majesty and your august highnesses, by the mercies of God, to listen with favor to the defense of a cause which I am well assured is just and right. I ask pardon, if by reason of my ignorance, I am wanting in the manners that befit a court; for I have not been brought up in kings' palaces, but in the seclusion of a cloister.

_____
_____

Problems 14–15: Read the excerpt in Appendix A from Jonathan Edwards's sermon "Sinners in the Hand of an Angry God," and answer the following questions.

14. Explain how in his sermon Edwards employs each of the given elements of the definition of fear.

   pain or disturbance _____
   _____
   _____

   due to a mental picture _____
   _____
   _____
   _____
   _____

   of destructive or painful evil _____
   _____
   _____
   _____
   _____

   in the future _____
   _____
   _____
   _____
   _____

15. Aristotle adds that "we know that we shall die, but we are not troubled thereby, because death is not close at hand." How does Edwards make death appear close at hand?

EXERCISE 13

NAME _____

DATE _____

Problems 1–12: Identify the emotion(s) from this lesson (shame, kindness, pity, indignation, envy, emulation) that the given speaker was seeking to produce in his hearers.

1. Genesis 34:21–23 _____
2. Deuteronomy 32:10–15 _____
3. Joshua 14:6–12 _____
4. Judges 5:24–27 _____
5. Ruth 1:11–13 _____
6. 1 Samuel 26:15–16 _____
7. Nehemiah 2:5–8 _____
8. Esther 8:5–6 _____
9. Proverbs 9:13–17 _____
10. Matthew 21:33–40 _____
11. John 8:42–47 _____
12. 2 Timothy 4:6–8 _____

Problems 13–15: The same speech may produce different emotions in different hearers. Read this excerpt from Martin Luther King Jr.'s speech *I Have a Dream*, and describe the type of hearer that would respond with the stated emotion. Explain your answer.

> Five score years ago, a great American, in whose symbolic shadow we stand today, signed the Emancipation Proclamation. This momentous decree came as a great beacon light of hope to millions of Negro slaves, who had been seared in the flames of withering injustice. It came as a joyous daybreak to end the long night of their captivity. But one hundred years later, the Negro still is not free. One hundred years later, the life of the Negro is still sadly crippled by the manacles of segregation and the chains of discrimination. One hundred years later, the Negro lives on a lonely island of

39

poverty in the midst of a vast ocean of material prosperity. One hundred years later, the Negro still languishes in the corners of American society and finds himself an exile in his own land.

13. Pity

14. Shame

15. Indignation

16. Select one of the emotions from Lesson 12 or 13, and write a portion of a speech seeking to produce that emotion in your hearers. Consider writing on the thesis you developed in Exercise 5. Identify at the end the intended emotion.

Intended Emotion: _____

EXERCISE 14A

NAME

DATE

Read 2 Samuel, chapters 11 and 12, and answer the following questions.

1. Explain why Nathan's speech (2 Samuel 12:1–12) is an example of *forensic oratory* (consider the description of forensic oratory from the third paragraph of this lesson).

   _____
   _____
   _____
   _____
   _____
   _____

2. Of what two wrongs does Nathan accuse David? Choose one, and explain how it fits the elements of the definition of *wrongdoing*.

   _____
   _____
   _____
   _____
   _____
   _____
   _____
   _____
   _____

3. Explain how David had the *opportunity* to commit adultery with Bathsheba.

4. Explain how David had the *means* to murder Uriah.

5. What pleasure(s) provided David's primary *motive* for these wrongs?

6. What was David's state of mind when committing these wrongs?

Fitting Words: Workbook | EXERCISE 14A

7. Why was David's murder of Uriah a *greater wrong* than a typical murder?

8. To which primary *class of victim* did Bathsheba and Uriah each belong?

9. David did not try to defend himself, but simply confessed and repented. What might a lesser man have said in defense of himself, appealing to *equity*?

EXERCISE 14B

NAME

DATE

Read Cicero's First Oration against Catiline, and answer the following questions. Defend your answers.

1. Explain why Cicero's speech is an example of *forensic oratory* (consider the description of forensic oratory from the third paragraph of this lesson).

2. Name three wrongs (or planned wrongs) for which Cicero accuses Catiline. Choose one, and explain how it fits the elements of the definition of *wrongdoing* (use the same wrong act for questions 3–5).

3. Explain how Catiline had or hoped to have the *means* to commit this wrong.

4. What pleasure(s) provided Catiline's *motive* for committing these wrongs?

5. What was Catiline's primary *state of mind* when committing this wrong?

6. To which *class of victim* did Cicero belong in regard to Catiline's attempted murder of him?

7. Name three techniques that Cicero uses to argue that Catiline's acts were a *greater wrong*?

8. Which of the *nontechnical means of persuasion* does Cicero employ in this speech?

EXERCISE 15A

NAME

DATE

Problems 1–2: Read through Christ's Sermon on the Mount, Matthew 5–7, and answer the following questions.

1. Appeal to the definition of political oratory to explain why this is a political speech. Defend your answer with biblical references.

2. Identify ten distinct good things (not necessarily from Aristotle's list) promised in this speech to those who faithfully obey God. Include references.

Problems 3–4: Read Exodus 18:13–23, and answer the following questions.

3. What does Jethro, Moses' father-in-law, urge him not to do because of harm? What does he urge him to do out of expediency?

4. To which *admittedly* good thing does Jethro appeal? To which *disputably* good thing? Defend your answers.

Problems 5–9: Read Deuteronomy 30:11–20, and answer the following questions.

5. Appeal to the definition of political oratory to explain why this is a political speech. Defend your answer with references.

   _____
   _____
   _____
   _____
   _____
   _____
   _____
   _____
   _____
   _____

6. Which of Aristotle's *definitions of happiness* could one argue that Moses is appealing to? Explain.

   _____
   _____
   _____
   _____
   _____
   _____

7. Which of Aristotle's *constituent parts of happiness* could one argue that Moses is appealing to? Defend your answer with references.

   _____
   _____
   _____
   _____
   _____
   _____

8. Other than the constituent parts of happiness, which primary *admittedly good thing* does Moses appeal to? Defend your answer with references.

9. Which *disputably good things* does Moses appeal to? Defend your answer with references.

EXERCISE 15B

NAME

DATE

Read "Give Me Liberty" by Patrick Henry, and answer the following questions. Defend your answers with appropriate quotations from the speech.

1. Which *definition of happiness* does Patrick Henry most appeal to?

2. Identify two or three *constituent parts of happiness* that Henry argues his hearers will gain.

3. Which of the *definitions of goodness* does Henry appear to have in mind in this speech?

4. In his final paragraph, Patrick Henry argues that one good is greater than another. Name these *contrasting goods*, and identify one of Aristotle's greater goods that support Henry's position.

EXERCISE 16A

NAME

DATE

Read this excerpt in praise of Isaac Newton from Petr Beckmann's *A History of Pi*, chapter 13, and answer the questions. Defend each of your answers using quotes from the excerpt.

> There had never been a scientist like Newton, and there has not been one like him since. Not Einstein, not Archimedes, not Galileo, not Planck, not anybody else measured up to anywhere near his stature. Indeed, it is safe to say that there can never be a scientist like Newton again, for the scientists of future generations will have books and libraries, microfilms and microfiches, magnetic discs and other computerized information to draw on. Newton had nothing, nothing except Galileo's qualitative thoughts and Kepler's laws of planetary motion. With little more than that to go on, Newton formulated three laws that govern all motion in the universe: From the galaxies in the heavens to the electrons whirling round atomic nuclei, from the cat that always falls on its feet to the gyroscopes that watch over the flight of space ships. His laws of motion have withstood the test of time for three centuries. The very concepts of space, time and mass have crumbled under the impact of Einstein's theory of relativity; age-old prejudices of cause, effect and certainty were destroyed by quantum mechanics; but Newton's laws have come through unscathed….
>
> Newton's achievement in discovering the differential and integral calculus is, in comparison, a smaller achievement; even so, it was epochal. As we have seen, the ground was well prepared for its discovery by a sizable troop of pioneers. Leibniz discovered it independently of Newton some ten years later, and Newton would not have been the giant he was if he had overlooked it. For Newton overlooked nothing. He found all the big things that were to be found in his time, and a host of lesser things (such as a way to calculate pi) as well. How many more his ever-brooding mind discovered, we shall never know, for he had an almost obsessive aversion to publishing his works. The greatest scientific book ever published, his Principia, took definite shape in his mind in 1665, when he was 23; but he did not commit his theories to paper until 1672–74. Whether he wrote them down for his own satisfaction or for posterity, we do not know, but the manuscript (of Part 1) lay in his drawer for ten more years, until his friend Edmond Halley

(1656–1742) accidentally learned of its existence in 1684. Halley was one of the world's great astronomers; yet his greatest contribution to science was persuading Newton to publish the Principia, urging him to finish the second and third parts, seeing them through the press, and financing their publication. In 1687 this greatest of all scientific works came off the press and heralded the birth of modern science.

Isaac Newton was born on Christmas Day, 1642, in a small farm house at Woolsthorpe near Colsterworth, Lincolnshire. At Grantham, the nearest place that had a school, he did not excel in mathematics in the dazzling way of the wonderchildren Pascal or Gauss, but his schoolmaster, Mr. Stokes, noticed that the boy was bright. If there was any omen of young Isaac's future destiny, it must have been his habit of brooding. Going home from Grantham, it was usual to dismount and lead one's horse up a particularly steep hill. But Isaac would occasionally be so deeply lost in meditation that he would forget to remount his horse and walk home the rest of the way.

When he finished school, there came the great turning point of Newton's career. His widowed mother wanted him to take over the farm, but Stokes was able to persuade her to send Isaac to Cambridge, where he was very quickly through with Euclid, and soon he mastered Descartes' new geometry. By the time he was twenty-one, he had discovered the binomial theorem for fractional powers, and had embarked on his discovery of infinite series and "fluxions" (derivatives). Soon he was correcting, and adding to, the work of his professor and friend, Isaac Barrow. In 1665 the Great Plague broke out, in Cambridge as well as London, and the university was closed down. Newton returned to Woolsthorpe for the rest of the year and part of the next. It is most probable that during this time, when he was twenty-three, with no one about but his mother to disturb his brooding, Newton made the greater part of his vast discoveries. "All this was in the two plague years 1665 and 1666," he reminisced in old age, "for in those days I was in the prime of my age of invention, and minded mathematics and [natural] philosophy more than at any time since." Asked how he made his discoveries, he answered, "By always thinking unto them," and on another occasion, "I keep the subject constantly before me and wait till the first dawnings open little by little into the full light." Newton retained these great powers of concentration throughout his life. He succeeded Barrow as Lucasian Professor of Mathematics at Cambridge (1669), and relinquished this post to become Warden of the Mint (1696) and later (1699) Master of the Mint; in 1703 he was elected President of the Royal Society, a position which he held until his death in 1726. In his later years he spent much time on non-scientific activity, but remained

Fitting Words: Workbook | EXERCISE 16A

as astute a mathematician as ever, amazing men by the ease with which he solved problems set up to challenge him.

In 1697, for example, Jean Bernoulli I (1667–1748) posed a problem that was to become famous in the founding of the Calculus of Variations: What is the curve joining two given points such that a heavy particle will move along the curve from the upper to the lower point in minimum time? The problem is so difficult that it is not, for example, usually included in today's under-graduate engineering curriculum. It was received by the Royal Society and handed to Newton in the afternoon; he returned the solution the next morning, and according to John Conduitt (his niece's husband), he solved it before going to bed! The solution was sent to Jean Bernoulli without signature, but on reading it he instantly recognized the author, as he exclaimed, *tanquam ex ungue leonem* (as the lion is known by its claw).

1. Which of Aristotle's forms of virtue does Beckmann primarily employ in praise of Newton?

2. Beckmann praises Newton using many of the noble deeds identified by Aristotle. Identify eight of them.

Problems 3–8: Beckmann also uses many methods to improve on his praise of Newton by pointing out how he was unique. Quote from the excerpt where he uses each given method.

3. He is the first one

Fitting Words: Workbook | EXERCISE 16A   **61**

4. He is the only one

5. He has done it better than anyone else

6. He has succeeded in this same way often

7. Unexpected success given the circumstances

8. Compare him with great men

EXERCISE 16B

NAME _____

DATE _____

Read this speech in praise of Gerhard Groote by Dr. George Grant[1] and answer the questions. Defend each of your answers using quotes from the speech.

Some men's greatness may be seen in how largely they loom over the movements they launched. But greater men are they whose movements loom large over them—even to the point of obscuring them from view.

Gerhard Groote was just such a man. It would be difficult to find a single page of modern history written about him. But it would be even more difficult to find a single page of modern history that has not been profoundly affected by him. He lived in the tumultuous days of the fourteenth century. A contemporary of John Wycliffe, Geoffrey Chaucer, and Jan Hus, he saw the scourge of the Black Death sweep a quarter of the population of the world away in a wave of pestilence; he saw France and England locked in the intractable conflagration of the Hundred Years War; he saw the Western church sundered by the Great Schism that produced two, sometimes three, sometimes even four, popes; and he saw the rise of the universities and the smothering influence of humanistic scholasticism. Churches were riven by corruption, kingdoms were shaken by instability, families were splintered by adversity, and the very foundations of Christian civilization in the West seemed to be crumbling.

They were dire days indeed. The problems facing men and nations seemed all but insurmountable. Doomsayers had a heyday. Sound familiar?

Groote was raised in the home of a prosperous merchant and received the finest education available. Alas, he found it difficult to take the claims of his academic masters, his ecclesiastical mentors, and his church peers seriously. Like so many of his contemporaries, he concluded that the overt wickedness of the church and the blatant debauchery of the university mitigated against any serious belief in the gospel. As a result, he ran from conviction and spent his youth and his wealth on reckless and heedless dissipation. He moved progressively from spoiled brat to party animal to insufferable boor. When he was finally arrested by grace and converted, he had tasted all the pleasures the medieval world had to offer—and still he yearned for more.

1 From Ligonier Ministries and R.C. Sproul. © *Tabletalk* magazine. Website: www.ligonier.org/tabletalk. Email: tabletalk@ligonier.org. Toll free: 1-800-435-4343. Used with permission.

63

As an ardent new convert in the midst of a church awash in promiscuous impiety, he lifted up an urgent prophetic voice against the evils of his day. He began to model a life of radical discipleship. And he attracted a strong following in his native Dutch lowlands.

Eventually, Groote's movement came to be known as the Brethren of the Common Life. He and his followers were committed to the authority of the Scriptures first and foremost. They promoted biblical preaching that was practical and accessible to the ordinary Christian. They pioneered vernacular translations of the Bible. And they founded schools to educate young men and women to be wise and discerning believers as well as effective and successful citizens.

The revival wrought by the movement was genuine, vibrant, and even widely admired. Even so, it could hardly have been expected to put a dent in the overwhelming problems of the day. Indeed, the litany of fourteenth century woes continued, seemingly unabated. When Groote died, some asserted that his efforts at renewal were ultimately stymied by the fierce reality of the circumstances of the day; he was by all such accounts, a failure.

But throughout his life and ministry, Groote was laying foundations for something that might endure well beyond his own life and ministry. He had a multigenerational plan. He understood that it had taken a very long time for Western civilization to get into the mess that it was in and that no man or movement, no matter how potent or effective, would be able to turn things around overnight. That was why the heart and soul of his plan was to disseminate the Scriptures and build schools. His covenantal theology had led him to have a generational vision, one that enabled him to invest in a future he would likely never see on this earth.

It was a wise strategy. Amazingly, in less than a century and a half the strategy began to bear abundant fruit: it was in those scattered and seemingly insignificant Brethren of Common Life schools that nearly every one of the magisterial reformers would ultimately be educated: Luther, Zwingli, Calvin, Melancthon, Bucer, and Beza.

An obscure man changed the course of history—albeit generations later—by simply living out the implications of radical grace and covenantal faithfulness right where he was. He faced the impossible odds of a culture gone terribly awry. He implemented a generational vision that laid new foundations for freedom and prosperity simply by equipping and enabling future leaders.

Perhaps by looking back at Groote and his reforming work, we will be able to see our way forward for our own. After all, his was a distinctly biblical vision, a sound vision, and thus a rather unpopular vision. And it still is.

Fitting Words: Workbook | EXERCISE 16B 65

1. Identify two of Aristotle's forms of virtue that Grant employs in praise of Groote.

2. Identify eight of the noble deeds identified by Aristotle that Grant uses in praise of Groote.

Problems 3–6: Grant also uses many methods to improve on his praise of Groote by pointing out how he was unique. Quote from the excerpt where he uses each given method.

3. He is the first one

4. He has done it better than anyone else

5. He has succeeded in this same way often

6. Unexpected success given the circumstances

7. In a couple of places Grant connects his praise of Groote with modern times, creating in his audience a spirit of emulation. Does this improve the effectiveness of his praise? Compare this method with Beckmann's approach to praising Isaac Newton.

EXERCISE 17A

NAME

DATE

Problems 1–3: For each of the given terms, identify at least three *parts* (or elements or steps) in the left column, and at least three *species* in the right column. Be careful to use consistent dividing principles.

1. Speech

   _____   _____
   _____   _____
   _____   _____

2. Sound

   _____   _____
   _____   _____
   _____   _____

3. Dinner

   _____   _____
   _____   _____
   _____   _____

4. Define *monarchy* in the following ways:

   Example _____

   _____

   Etymology _____

   _____

   Genus and difference _____

   _____

Problems 5–6: Read through Patrick Henry's "Give Me Liberty" speech (see Appendix A of the text), then answer the questions, quoting the appropriate passage from the speech.

5. What term does Henry define (or clarify) with repeated synonyms? List the synonyms.

   _____
   _____
   _____

6. Henry defined "to be free" with a genus and difference definition. What other term does he clarify by providing a genus and difference definition? What is his definition?

   _____
   _____
   _____

EXERCISE 17B

NAME

DATE

Read this excerpt from Martin Luther King Jr.'s Letter from Birmingham Jail, and answer the questions.

> I think I should indicate why I am here in Birmingham, since you have been influenced by the view which argues against "outsiders coming in."… Several months ago the affiliate here in Birmingham asked us to be on call to engage in a nonviolent direct action program if such were deemed necessary. We readily consented, and when the hour came we lived up to our promise. So I, along with several members of my staff, am here because I was invited here. I am here because I have organizational ties here.
>
> But more basically, I am in Birmingham because injustice is here. Just as the prophets of the eighth century B.C. left their villages and carried their "thus saith the Lord" far beyond the boundaries of their home towns, and just as the Apostle Paul left his village of Tarsus and carried the gospel of Jesus Christ to the far corners of the Greco Roman world, so am I compelled to carry the gospel of freedom beyond my own home town. Like Paul, I must constantly respond to the Macedonian call for aid.
>
> Moreover, I am cognizant of the interrelatedness of all communities and states. I cannot sit idly by in Atlanta and not be concerned about what happens in Birmingham. Injustice anywhere is a threat to justice everywhere. We are caught in an inescapable network of mutuality, tied in a single garment of destiny. Whatever affects one directly, affects all indirectly. Never again can we afford to live with the narrow, provincial "outside agitator" idea. Anyone who lives inside the United States can never be considered an outsider anywhere within its bounds….

1. The word "outsider" is vague. How would the opponents of Dr. King define this term? How does he redefine this term? Explain how his redefinition helps to make his rhetorical point.

_____

_____

_____

_____
_____
_____
_____
_____
_____
_____
_____
_____
_____

Now do the same for this excerpt.

> In any nonviolent campaign there are four basic steps: collection of the facts to determine whether injustices exist; negotiation; self-purification; and direct action. We have gone through all these steps in Birmingham. There can be no gainsaying the fact that racial injustice engulfs this community. Birmingham is probably the most thoroughly segregated city in the United States. Its ugly record of brutality is widely known. Negroes have experienced grossly unjust treatment in the courts. There have been more unsolved bombings of Negro homes and churches in Birmingham than in any other city in the nation. These are the hard, brutal facts of the case. On the basis of these conditions, Negro leaders sought to negotiate with the city fathers. But the latter consistently refused to engage in good faith negotiation….
>
> Mindful of the difficulties involved, we decided to undertake a process of self-purification. We began a series of workshops on nonviolence, and we repeatedly asked ourselves: "Are you able to accept blows without retaliating?" "Are you able to endure the ordeal of jail?" We decided to schedule our direct action program for the Easter season, realizing that except for Christmas, this is the main shopping period of the year. Knowing that a strong economic-withdrawal program would be the by-product of direct action, we felt that this would be the best time to bring pressure to bear on the merchants for the needed change….

Fitting Words: Workbook | EXERCISE 17B   73

2. Dr. King identifies four steps of a nonviolent campaign. Explain how each step leads to the next.

___

Read this final excerpt, and answer the questions.

> You express a great deal of anxiety over our willingness to break laws. This is certainly a legitimate concern. Since we so diligently urge people to obey the Supreme Court's decision of 1954 outlawing segregation in the public schools, at first glance it may seem rather paradoxical for us consciously to break laws. One may well ask: "How can you advocate breaking some laws and obeying others?" The answer lies in the fact that there are two types of laws: just and unjust. I would be the first to advocate obeying just laws. One has not only a legal but a moral responsibility to obey just laws. Conversely, one has a moral responsibility to disobey unjust laws. I would agree with St. Augustine that "an unjust law is no law at all."
>
> Now, what is the difference between the two? How does one determine whether a law is just or unjust? A just law is a man-made code that squares with the moral law or the law of God. An unjust law is a code that is out of harmony with the moral law. To put it in the terms of St. Thomas Aquinas: An unjust law is a human law that is not rooted in eternal law and natural law. Any law that uplifts human personality is just. Any law that degrades human personality is unjust...Thus it is that I can urge men to obey the

1954 decision of the Supreme Court, for it is morally right; and I can urge them to disobey segregation ordinances, for they are morally wrong....

Of course, there is nothing new about this kind of civil disobedience. It was evidenced sublimely in the refusal of Shadrach, Meshach and Abednego to obey the laws of Nebuchadnezzar, on the ground that a higher moral law was at stake. It was practiced superbly by the early Christians, who were willing to face hungry lions and the excruciating pain of chopping blocks rather than submit to certain unjust laws of the Roman Empire. To a degree, academic freedom is a reality today because Socrates practiced civil disobedience. In our own nation, the Boston Tea Party represented a massive act of civil disobedience...

3. What are the two species of law that Dr. King identifies? Identify three dividing principles he uses to distinguish them.

_____
_____
_____
_____
_____
_____
_____
_____

EXERCISE 18A

Problems 1–8: Identify the statements as *simple* or *compound* by circling the correct choice.

1. We are met on a great battlefield of that war.

    simple   compound

2. The world will little note, nor long remember, what we say here.

    simple   compound

3. There is a just God who presides over the destinies of nations.

    simple   compound

4. An appeal to arms and to the God of hosts is all that is left us!

    simple   compound

5. I will prove it if you do deny it.

    simple   compound

6. The consul orders an enemy to depart from the city.

    simple   compound

7. Injustice anywhere is a threat to justice everywhere.

    simple   compound

8. Time can be used either destructively or constructively.

    simple   compound

Problems 9–13: Write whether the statements from the Bible are *singular* or *indefinite*. If they are indefinite, write whether the statement should be considered *particular* or *universal*.

9. The rulers take counsel together against the Lord and against His Anointed. (Psalm 2:2)

10. Righteousness exalts a nation. (Proverbs 14:34)

11. Babylon has caused the slain of Israel to fall. (Jeremiah 51:49)

12. The lamp of the body is the eye. (Matthew 6:22)

13. The dead were judged according to their works. (Revelation 20:12)

EXERCISE 18B

1. Read Acts 26:25–32 below. Identify each **bold** compound statement as a *conjunction, disjunction,* or *conditional*.

   ²⁵ "I am not insane, most excellent Festus," Paul replied. "**What I am saying is true and reasonable**. ²⁶ The king is familiar with these things, and I can speak freely to him. I am convinced that none of this has escaped his notice, because it was not done in a corner. ²⁷ King Agrippa, do you believe the prophets? I know you do."

   ²⁸ Then Agrippa said to Paul, "Do you think that in such a short time you can persuade me to be a Christian?"

   ²⁹ Paul replied, "Short time or long— **I pray to God that not only you but all who are listening to me today may become what I am**, except for these chains."

   ³⁰ The king rose, and with him the governor and Bernice and those sitting with them. ³¹ After they left the room, they began saying to one another, "**This man is not doing anything that deserves death or imprisonment**."

   ³² Agrippa said to Festus, "**This man could have been set free if he had not appealed to Caesar**."

Problems 2–3: Combine the two statements by rewriting them into a single *biconditional*. (Ignore minor additional details and different wording. Write in normal sounding language.)

2. "If you surely surrender to the king of Babylon's princes, then your soul shall live; this city shall not be burned with fire, and you and your house shall live. But if you do not surrender to the king of Babylon's princes, then this city shall be given into the hand of the Chaldeans; they shall burn it with fire, and you shall not escape from their hand" (Jeremiah 38:17–18).

   _____
   _____
   _____

3. "For if you forgive men their trespasses, your heavenly Father will also forgive you. But if you do not forgive men their trespasses, neither will your Father forgive your trespasses" (Matthew 6:14–15).

   _____
   _____
   _____

Problems 4–12: Identify the most specific relationship between the given pair of statements from this list: *contradiction, contrariety, equivalence, implication, independence, subcontrariety*.

4. All mechanical things break. / Some mechanical things do not break.

   _____

5. Some mathematicians are engineers. / Some engineers are mathematicians.

   _____

6. Everybody loves a winner. / Nobody loves a winner.

   _____

Fitting Words: Workbook | EXERCISE 18B

7. Sometimes you just can't win. / Sometimes you can win.

8. This man Zechariah has a son. / This man Zechariah is a father.

9. Jane is a wife. / Jane has a sister-in-law.

10. Some desperados are renegades. / No desperados are renegades.

11. Martin is neither a priest nor a soldier. / Martin is not a soldier.

12. He is a good director if and only if he is an experienced actor. / He is an experienced actor.

13. Identify by problem number (4–12) which of the above pair of statements are consistent. _____

EXERCISE 19A

NAME

DATE

For each given statement from the Declaration of Independence, identify the method by which the author Thomas Jefferson came to know the truth of it. Be specific. You may add a brief explanation for your answer. Also, you may be assisted by reading the statements in context.

1. "All men are created equal."

   _____
   _____
   _____

2. "Governments long established should not be changed for light and transient causes."

   _____
   _____
   _____
   _____

3. "The history of the present king of Great Britain is a history of repeated injuries and usurpations, all having in direct object the establishment of an absolute tyranny over these States."

   _____
   _____
   _____

4. "He has kept among us, in times of peace, standing armies."

   _____
   _____
   _____

5. "He has constrained our fellow citizens taken captive on the high seas to bear arms against their country."

6. "These United Colonies are, and of right ought to be free and independent states."

EXERCISE 19B

Problems 1–4: Argue for the truth of the given statement by appealing to an equivalent statement, identified as *converse, obverse,* or *contrapositive* (use each at least once). Use ordinary language.

1. All His ways are justice. (Deuteronomy 32:4)

2. No one who puts his hand to the plow and looks back is fit for the kingdom of God. (Luke 9:62)

3. Some of the king's servants are dead. (2 Samuel 11:24)

4. Some disciples do not believe. (John 6:64)

Problems 5–10: For the given statement, write a different but equivalent statement.

5. You shall not kill both the cow and her young on the same day. (Leviticus 22:28)

6. You have neither heard His voice at any time, nor seen His form. (John 5:37)

7. If that first covenant had been faultless, then no place would have been sought for a second. (Hebrews 8:7)

8. The law is good if one uses it lawfully. (1 Timothy 1:8)

9. Unless one is born again, he cannot see the kingdom of God. (John 3:3)

10. If, while her husband lives, she marries another man, she is an adulteress; but if her husband dies, she is no adulteress, though she has married another man. (Romans 7:3)

Problems 11–14: Use the given general line of argument to argue for the given statement. Write the argument in if–then form, with the given statement as the consequent.

11. He who does good unwittingly does not deserve a reward. (Opposites)

12. The church is free to use the congregation's tithes as they see fit. (Correlative ideas)

13. Schools must allow boys to join the volleyball team. (Rational correspondence)

14. It is wrong to slander your friends. (*A fortiori*)

EXERCISE 20

NAME _____

DATE _____

Problems 1–4: For each type of maxim, give an example along with a brief explanation of why the maxim is of that type. You may find your own or select them from the list of 100 maxims.

1. Known truth _____
   _____
   _____
   _____
   _____
   _____
   _____
   _____

2. Clear at a glance _____
   _____
   _____
   _____
   _____
   _____
   _____
   _____

3. Paradoxical _____
   _____
   _____
   _____
   _____
   _____
   _____
   _____

4. Disputable _____

5. Give an example, different from the above, of two maxims from the list of 100 that appear to contradict. Explain how the maxims can be reconciled by a proper understanding of the context.

6. Give examples of biblical maxims, one from the Old Testament and one from the New, which would be familiar to people who have not read the Bible. Include the references.

7. Develop an enthymeme (an argument of one premise and one conclusion) by taking a maxim from the list of 100 and adding a brief explanation.

8. Rewrite a maxim by removing some words. The new maxim must still make sense.

9. Refute a disputable maxim from the list of 100, adding an explanation of why it is wrong in the case supposed.

EXERCISE 21A

NAME

DATE

Problems 1–3: Read this excerpt, an argument from actual past fact, from Martin Luther's *Here I Stand*, and answer the given questions.

> Let us have a care lest the reign of the young and noble prince, the emperor Charles, on whom, next to God, we build so many hopes, should not only commence, but continue and terminate its course under the most fatal auspices. I might cite examples drawn from the oracles of God. I might speak of pharaohs, of kings of Babylon, or of Israel, who were never more contributing to their own ruin that when, by measures in appearances most prudent, they thought to establish their authority!

1. Explain how the examples cited are relevantly similar to the point Luther is making.

   _____
   _____
   _____
   _____
   _____
   _____
   _____
   _____
   _____

2. Locate a scriptural reference where each king from Luther's examples contributed to his ruin by seeking to establish his authority.

   Pharaoh of Egypt _____
   King of Babylon _____
   King of Israel _____

91

3. By means of these examples, Luther subtly sides with the biblical heroes who opposed each of these kings. Identify the man he is likely identifying with who opposed each given king.

Pharaoh of Egypt _____

King of Babylon _____

King of Israel _____

Problems 4–5: Read this excerpt from Jonathan Edwards's sermon "Sinners in the Hand of an Angry God," and answer the given questions. (Line numbers are added for convenience.)

> ¹It is no security to wicked men for one moment, that there are no visible means of death at hand. ²It is no security to a natural man, that he is now in health, and that he does not see which way he should now immediately go out of the world by any accident, and that there is no visible danger in any respect in his circumstances. ³The manifold and continual experience of the world in all ages, shows this is no evidence, that a man is not on the very brink of eternity, and that the next step will not be into another world. ⁴The unseen, unthought-of ways and means of persons going suddenly out of the world are innumerable and inconceivable. ⁵Unconverted men walk over the pit of hell on a rotten covering, and there are innumerable places in this covering so weak that they will not bear their weight, and these places are not seen. ⁶The arrows of death fly unseen at noon-day; the sharpest sight cannot discern them. ⁷God has so many different unsearchable ways of taking wicked men out of the world and sending them to hell, that there is nothing to make it appear, that God had need to be at the expense of a miracle, or go out of the ordinary course of his providence, to destroy any wicked man, at any moment.

This excerpt contains two illustrative parallels. For each one identified, write out the source example and target conclusion behind the illustrative parallel.

4. From line 5

   Source _____
   _____
   _____

Target _____

5. From line 6

Source _____

Target _____

EXERCISE 21B

NAME _____

DATE _____

Problems 1–4: For the three types of argument by example, come up with a single thesis statement that could be supported by them. Then write out each of the three types of argument. You may again use your thesis statement from Exercise 5 if it has the quality of a maxim.

1. Thesis _____
   _____
   _____
   _____

2. Mention of actual past fact _____
   _____
   _____
   _____
   _____
   _____
   _____

3. Illustrative parallel _____
   _____
   _____
   _____
   _____
   _____
   _____

4. Fable

EXERCISE 22A

Problems 1–8: Underline the conclusion in the given categorical syllogism. These syllogisms will also be used for problems 9–16.

1. Given that all postmillennialists are preterists, and some postmillennialists are Presbyterians, it follows that <u>some Presbyterians are preterists</u>.

2. <u>Some loving fathers are not stay-at-home dads</u>, because no loving fathers abandon their children, and no stay-at-home dads abandon their children.

3. All first-degree murderers are felons. Consequently, <u>some first-degree murderers are thieves</u>, because some felons are thieves.

4. All categorical syllogisms are logical arguments, and all logical arguments are things made up of words. Thus, <u>some things made up of words are not categorical syllogisms</u>.

5. <u>Some quadrilaterals are squares</u>, for all rectangles are quadrilaterals, and all squares are rectangles.

6. <u>Some exogenous chemicals are synthesized from amino acids</u>, since no neurotransmitters are exogenous chemicals, and some neurotransmitters are synthesized from amino acids.

7. No Shakespearian dramas are epic poems, but some Shakespearian dramas are histories. Therefore, <u>some histories are not epic poems</u>.

8. All people who want to be continually reelected are career politicians, so <u>some pathological liars are not career politicians</u>, since no one who wants to be continually reelected is a pathological liar.

Problems 9–16: Determine whether the syllogism of the each of the problems above is valid or invalid. If it is invalid, explain the rule being broken.

9. #1 _____

_____

10. #2 _____

11. #3 _____

12. #4 _____

13. #5 _____

14. #6 _____

15. #7 _____

16. #8 _____

Problems 17–20: Develop a sound categorical syllogism with the given statement as the conclusion.

17. All great speakers were once bad speakers.

18. No true freedom is truly free.

19. Some Jews are Christians.

20. Some words are not fit to speak.

EXERCISE 22B

Problems 1–4: Write an enthymeme (complete proof) to establish the given conclusion. You may use the Aristotelian form "The fact that p is a sign that q" with the statement q as the conclusion.

1. "Your computer will eventually need to be replaced."

2. "Texting during a theater performance is rude."

3. "Men are inclined to evil when justice is delayed."

4. "True love does not fade with the beloved's absence."

5. Write a refutable sign that could be used to support one of the conclusions from problems 1–4.

6. Write a valid disjunctive syllogism with this conclusion: "You should read the entire Bible."

7. Write a pure hypothetical syllogism with this conclusion: "If you love your country, then you will fight to defend it."

8. Write a *modus ponens* with this conclusion: "Stories are an effective means of teaching."

9. Write a *modus tollens* with this conclusion: "Christians should not worry about the future."

10. Write a dilemma about deciding whether or not to buy a car.

11. Write a detailed argument on any topic. Include 1) a disjunctive syllogism, 2) a pure hypothetical syllogism, 3) a *modus ponens*, and 4) a *modus tollens*. Identify each by number in the margin.

EXERCISE 23A

NAME _____

DATE _____

Problems 1–2: Section 1 of the Fourteenth Amendment to the U.S. Constitution reads,

> All persons born or naturalized in the United States, and subject to the jurisdiction thereof, are citizens of the United States and of the State wherein they reside. No State shall make or enforce any law which shall abridge the privileges or immunities of citizens of the United States; *nor shall any State deprive any person of life, liberty, or property, without due process of law*; nor deny to any person within its jurisdiction the equal protection of the laws.

In *Roe v. Wade*, the court decided that the Fourteenth Amendment's use of the word *person* did not refer to the unborn, and that, therefore, a fetus has no constitutional right to life.

1. What definition could be given for the word *person* that is consistent with the court's decision in *Roe v. Wade*? (You may do some research to help answer this question.)

   _____
   _____
   _____
   _____

2. Define the word *person* in a way that could be used to refute the court's decision.

   _____
   _____
   _____
   _____
   _____

Problems 3–4: Read Patrick Henry's "Give Me Liberty" speech, and answer the questions.

3. Henry apparently refutes the following objection: "We should continue to petition the British ministry. They gave our recent petition a gracious reception." Summarize Henry's two distinct refutations to this objection.

4. Henry then refutes this objection: "We are weak. We could not win a war against Britain." Summarize Henry's refutation to this objection.

5. During Absalom's rebellion in 2 Samuel 17, Ahithophel counsels Absalom to attack David at once (vv. 1–3), but Hushai counsels him to wait (vv. 8–13). Identify two key arguments by probability they use that completely differ between them.

6. In 2 Kings 19:10–13, the Rabshakeh of the king of Assyria uses an inductive argument to try to persuade King Hezekiah that the Lord cannot save Jerusalem. Summarize the argument, and explain why it is a weak argument (consider verses 15–19).

EXERCISE 23B

NAME

DATE

Problems 1–8: Identify the conditional argument as *modus ponens* (MP), *modus tollens* (MT), affirming the consequent (AC), or denying the antecedent (DA). You may abbreviate.

1. If you do well, then your sacrifice will be accepted. But Cain did not do well. Consequently, his sacrifice was not accepted. _____

2. If I ascend into heaven, God is there. God is in heaven. Therefore, I have ascended into heaven. _____

3. If ten righteous men had been found, then the city would have been spared. The city was not spared, so ten righteous men must not have been found. _____

4. When the child was born a boy, he was to be killed. Moses was a son. Thus, Moses was to be killed. _____

5. If a thief is caught, then he is to restore double. That child was caught stealing, so she had to restore double. _____

6. If you want to live a godly life, then you will be persecuted. My friends and I are often persecuted. We must want to live godly lives. _____

7. If a ruler listens to lies, then all of his servants become wicked. Many of Solomon's servants were not wicked. Clearly, he did not listen to lies. _____

8. Mormon doctrine is true only if the Scripture mentions a third heaven. The Bible does mention a third heaven. Hence, Mormon doctrine is true. _____

109

Problems 9–13: Refute the given dilemma. Identify the method used: grasping the horns, going between the horns, or rebutting the horns. Use each of these three methods at least once.

9. If I try to teach a lot of concepts, then the lessons will be shallow. But if I try to teach only a few concepts, then I will not cover the subject completely. I try to teach a lot of concepts or only a few. Thus, my teaching is either shallow of incomplete.

   _____
   _____
   _____
   _____
   _____
   _____
   _____
   _____

   Name the method used: _____

10. If people are good, then laws are not needed to prevent wrongdoing, but if people are evil, then the laws are not able to prevent wrongdoing. People are either good or evil. Consequently, laws are either not needed or not able to prevent wrongdoing.

    _____
    _____
    _____
    _____
    _____
    _____
    _____
    _____

    Name the method used: _____

Fitting Words: Workbook | EXERCISE 23B 111

11. If the U.S. reduces carbon emissions, then our economy will be hampered. If we do not reduce carbon emissions, then we contribute to global warming. We either reduce carbon emissions or not, so either our economy is hampered or we contribute to global warming.

   _____
   _____
   _____
   _____
   _____
   _____
   _____
   _____

   Name the method used: _____

12. If Christians immerse themselves in modern culture, then they will be polluted by it. But for Christians to escape modern culture they must become hermits. Christians will either immerse themselves in modern culture or seek to escape it, so they will either be polluted by culture or they will become hermits.

   _____
   _____
   _____
   _____
   _____
   _____
   _____
   _____

   Name the method used: _____

13. If you love someone, then you will hurt them, and if you love no one, then you will be lonely. You will love someone or no one, so you will hurt someone or you will be lonely.

   Name the method used: _____

Problems 14–18: Write a counterexample to the given syllogism or enthymeme. Make sure that your premises are clearly true and that your conclusion is clearly false.

14. All good poems rhyme, for all Shakespeare's sonnets are good poems, and all of them rhyme.

15. All formaldehyde-based laminates emit unhealthy gases, but some laminates are not formaldehyde based. Therefore, some laminates don't emit unhealthy gases.

Fitting Words: Workbook | EXERCISE 23B 113

16. No writers of lewd articles are decent citizens, but some journalists are not writers of lewd articles. Therefore, some journalists are decent citizens.

17. Teenagers are not yet adults, because teenagers go to movies regularly.

18. Oswald must have been the lone assassin of Kennedy. After all, it's been over fifty years and nobody has proven that anyone else helped him.

Problems 19–20: Write a *reductio ad absurdum* argument to refute the given claim.

19. If you die when you are dreaming, then you die in reality and never wake up.

20. Words cannot convey meaning.

EXERCISE 24A

NAME

DATE

Explain what the two fallacies have in common, then explain how they differ.

1. Bandwagon fallacy / *Ad misericordiam*

2. False analogy / Straw man

3. Hasty generalization / Composition

4. Equivocation / Amphiboly

5. Cherry-picking / Accident

EXERCISE 24B

Identify the informal fallacy being made. Be specific.

1. "No individual vote in an election makes a worthwhile difference, so elections are a worthless means of making public choices."

2. "A large percentage of the voting public report that they plan to vote for Senator West, so she is clearly the best candidate."

3. "We wanted to hear from the student body about fun activities, so we asked the senior girls, and they all said we should have a formal dance. So that's what we should do."

4. "You think that the school should have a formal dance just because you are a dance instructor!"

5. "My sister says I shouldn't flirt with the lifeguard at the pool, but I have seen her talking with the guys at the café, so why should I listen to her?"

6. "What's wrong with flirting with that lifeguard? Swimming is a healthy activity, and should get me in shape for running cross country!"

7. "Yes, officer, I know about the ordinance not to leave dogs in a car in hot weather. But I wasn't *leaving* my dog, I was just going into the store and then coming back."

_____

8. "Officer, it wouldn't be right to fine me for leaving my dog. I have had such a hard day, my husband yelled at me this morning, my son has the flu, and it's my birthday!"

_____

9. "Why should we be confident that there is intelligent life on other planets? Because that biologist said so, and he even advocates trying to communicate with them."

_____

10. "You don't think that there are intelligent aliens in our galaxy? You must believe that earth is the only planet where biological life can exist!"

_____

11. "No one has proven that there is extraterrestrial life, so humans must indeed be alone."

_____

12. "The teachers at that college are all liberals, so when you go there to study, don't believe anything they say to you!"

_____

13. "My daughter's first year of college cost $18,000, and for what? English 101, a philosophy course, and an easy math class. Higher education is a waste of time and money!"

_____

14. "The human body is like a machine, and it's not wrong to turn off a machine after it's been running a long time. So it is acceptable to end the life of the sick and aged."

15. "If you continue advocating for death with dignity, some day you will be in a nursing home on life support, and they will end your life with no dignity at all!"

16. "You shouldn't play poker with chips. Next thing you know you'll be playing for money, then playing at the casino, then losing all you have until you are on the streets begging!"

17. "What's wrong with people begging? You are begging me to stop gambling!"

18. "Fathers should help their children with their studies, so I wrote my son's essay for him."

19. "Having students write thesis papers and defend them is a medieval practice that is not necessary in these modern times."

20. "It is morally wrong to use animals for medical testing. Imagine researchers gleefully injecting poisons into puppies, and poking their exposed brains just to see what happens!"

21. "America should not have stopped sending men to the moon. The last Apollo mission came back in December 1972, and what happened? In January 1973 we got *Roe v. Wade*."

_____

22. "We should continue to send astronauts to the moon because it would be beneficial for men to travel to the lunar surface."

_____

23. "You say I should learn good conversation skills because they will help me to be a good friend and to gain confidence. But there is so much more to learn: personal finances, auto repair, biblical Greek…"

_____

24. "I have heard that learning biblical Greek will take years of intensive study, so it will probably take a long time to learn the Greek alphabet."

_____

25. "A sign in the park read, 'If your dog messes on the grass, please dispose of it.' That sounds pretty harsh."

_____

26. "Have you stopped abusing your dog?"

_____

EXERCISE 25A

NAME

DATE

1. From the list of characteristics of the young versus the old, what emotion do you think would be the easiest to raise in young men? In old men? Briefly explain your answers.

2. Write two paragraphs urging this thesis: "Every man should own a truck." Aim the first paragraph at young men and the second paragraph at old men.

Fitting Words: Workbook | EXERCISE 25A

3. Write two paragraphs urging this thesis: "Parents should begin saving money for their children from birth." Aim the first paragraph at men, and the second paragraph at women.

EXERCISE 25B

NAME

DATE

1. Write two paragraphs arguing on one side or the other of this debate resolution: "It is right to keep animals in zoos." In the first paragraph, argue as a Christian, and the second paragraph, argue as an atheist.

EXERCISE 26A

NAME

DATE

Problems 1–3: Circle the nominalizations in the given sentences. Then improve their clarity by rewriting the sentences, turning nominalizations into their corresponding verbs and adjectives.

1. My father did his work for many hours of thanklessness in order to make provision for us.

2. Your inability to mount an attack against the Republic was due to the prevention of my guards.

3. The expense is significant for the construction and maintenance of power plants for the harnessing of wind energy.

4. Use appropriate nominalizations to make this sentence shorter and clearer: "The fact that he completely understood the situation helped him to be particularly insightful."

Problems 5–6: Read the following excerpt from Patrick Henry's "Give Me Liberty" (line numbers have been added):

> ¹ Sir, we have done everything that could be done to avert the storm which is now coming on. ² We have petitioned; we have remonstrated; we have supplicated; we have prostrated ourselves before the throne, and have implored its interposition to arrest the tyrannical hands of the ministry and Parliament. ³ Our petitions have been slighted; our remonstrances have produced additional violence and insult; our supplications have been disregarded; and we have been spurned, with contempt, from the foot of the throne! ⁴ In vain, after these things, may we indulge the fond hope of peace and reconciliation.

5. In line 2, Henry gives us a series of four statements regarding what the colonists have done, balanced in line 3 by four statements about the response of the king. Write out the statements with the corresponding acts of the colonists and responses of the king placed side by side.

6. Which voice, active or passive, is used to describe the actions of the colonists? Which is used to describe the response of the king? Explain why Henry used each voice as he did.

Fitting Words: Workbook | EXERCISE 26A

Problems 7–8: Read this excerpt from Martin Luther King Jr.'s Letter from Birmingham Jail:

> So I have not said to my people: 'Get rid of your discontent.' Rather, I have tried to say that this normal and healthy discontent can be channeled into the creative outlet of nonviolent direct action. And now this approach is being termed extremist.

7. The second and third sentences use the passive voice. Rewrite the whole section with every sentence being grammatically active (you will have to invent reasonable agents of the action).

8. Explain why the passive is the better choice for those sentences.

EXERCISE 26B

NAME

DATE

1. Rewrite this closing line of John F. Kennedy's Inaugural Address, removing as much as possible the rhythm and parallel structure.

   With a good conscience our only sure reward, with history the final judge of our deeds, let us go forth to lead the land we love, asking His blessing and His help, but knowing that here on earth God's work must truly be our own.

   _____
   _____
   _____
   _____
   _____
   _____
   _____
   _____

Problems 2–3: Follow the pattern of the analysis from the example at the end of the lesson to display the elegant structure of the given closing sentences. Because you will need extra room to maneuver, the questions are sideways on the next two pages.

2. "In short they have no refuge, nothing to take hold of; all that preserves them every moment is the mere arbitrary will, and uncovenanted, unobliged forbearance of an incensed God."

3. "If, then, I am not convinced by proof from Holy Scripture, or by cogent reasons, if I am not satisfied by the very text I have cited, and if my judgment is not in this way brought into subjection to God's word, I neither can nor will retract anything; for it cannot be right for a Christian to speak against his conscience."

EXERCISE 27A

NAME

DATE

Identify three figures of speech used in each of the given speech excerpts. Briefly explain each one to demonstrate your understanding of the figure.

1. "We Americans are vitally concerned in your defense of freedom. We are putting forth our energies, our resources, and our organizing powers to give you the strength to regain and maintain a free world. We shall send you in ever-increasing numbers, ships, planes, tanks, guns. That is our purpose and our pledge."—FDR, *Four Freedoms*

2. "Now is the time to make real the promises of democracy. Now is the time to rise from the dark and desolate valley of segregation to the sunlit path of racial justice. Now is the time to lift our nation from the quicksands of racial injustice to the solid rock of brotherhood. Now is the time to make justice a reality for all of God's children."—MLK, *I Have a Dream*

_____
_____
_____
_____
_____
_____
_____
_____
_____
_____
_____
_____
_____
_____

3. "So let us begin anew—remembering on both sides that civility is not a sign of weakness, and sincerity is always subject to proof. Let us never negotiate out of fear. But let us never fear to negotiate. Let both sides explore what problems unite us instead of belaboring those problems which divide us."—JFK, *Inaugural Address*

_____
_____
_____
_____
_____
_____

Fitting Words: Workbook | EXERCISE 27A

4. "And we know that all things work together for good to those who love God, to those who are the called according to His purpose. For whom He foreknew, He also predestined to be conformed to the image of His Son, that He might be the firstborn among many brethren. Moreover whom He predestined, these He also called; whom He called, these He also justified; and whom He justified, these He also glorified. What then shall we say to these things? If God is for us, who can be against us?"—Romans 8:28–31

5. "I have but one lamp by which my feet are guided, and that is the lamp of experience. I know of no way of judging of the future but by the past. And judging by the past, I wish to know what there has been in the conduct of the British ministry for the last ten years to justify those hopes with which gentlemen have been pleased to solace themselves and the House."—Patrick Henry, *Give Me Liberty*

   _____
   _____
   _____
   _____
   _____
   _____
   _____
   _____
   _____
   _____

6. "This day is called the feast of Crispian.
   He that outlives this day and comes safe home
   Will stand a tip-toe when the day is named
   And rouse him at the name of Crispian.
   He that shall live this day and see old age
   Will yearly on the vigil feast his neighbors,
   And say 'Tomorrow is Saint Crispian.'
   Then will he strip his sleeve and show his scars
   And say 'These wounds I had on Crispin's day.'
   Old men forget: yet all shall be forgot,
   But he'll remember with advantages
   What feats he did that day."
   —Henry V, *St. Crispin's Day*

EXERCISE 27B

NAME

DATE

Problems 1–5: Identify the primary figure of speech used in the given sentences. Then rewrite them in plain style, removing the figure of speech.

1. "The tablets were written on both sides; on the one side and on the other they were written. Now the tablets were the work of God, and the writing was the writing of God engraved on the tablets." (Exodus 32:15–16)

   _____
   _____
   _____
   _____

2. "…mankind are more disposed to suffer, while evils are sufferable, than to right themselves by abolishing the forms to which they are accustomed."— Declaration of Independence

   _____
   _____
   _____
   _____

3. "You shall love the Lord your God with all your heart, with all your soul, with all your strength, and with all your mind." (Luke 10:27)

   _____
   _____
   _____
   _____

4. "Bishops air their opinions about economics; biologists, about metaphysics; inorganic chemists, about theology."—Sayers, *The Lost Tools of Learning*

_____
_____
_____
_____
_____

5. "And the kings of the earth, and the great men, and the rich men, and the chief captains, and the mighty men, and every bondman, and every free man, hid themselves in the dens and in the rocks of the mountains." (Revelation 6:15)

_____
_____
_____
_____
_____

Problems 6–12: Rewrite or expand this sentence using a different figure of speech from this lesson each time. Identify the figure used. Be creative!

John climbed up the ladder in order to fix the leak in his roof.

6. _____
_____
_____

7. _____
_____
_____

8.
9.
10.
11.
12.

EXERCISE 28A

NAME

DATE

Problems 1–12: Identify the primary trope used in the given Bible verse. There is one each of the twelve tropes in the lesson.

1. "Would you plead for Baal? Would you save him? Let the one who would plead for him be put to death by morning!" (Judges 6:31)

   _____

2. "They were swifter than eagles, they were stronger than lions." (2 Samuel 1:23)

   _____

3. "For I will not trust in my bow, nor shall my sword save me." (Psalm 44:6)

   _____

4. "Wisdom calls aloud outside; she raises her voice in the open squares." (Proverbs 1:20)

   _____

5. "We are the clay, and You our potter; and all we are the work of Your hand." (Isaiah 64:8)

   _____

6. "I have raised My hand in an oath that surely the nations that are around you shall bear their own shame. But you, O mountains of Israel, you shall shoot forth your branches and yield your fruit to My people Israel, for they are about to come." (Ezekiel 36:7–8)

   _____

7. "For where your treasure is, there your heart will be also." (Matthew 6:21) _____

8. "Behold, I send you out as sheep in the midst of wolves. Therefore be wise as serpents and harmless as doves." (Matthew 10:16) _____

9. "What shall I do? For my master is taking the stewardship away from me. I cannot dig; I am ashamed to beg." (Luke 16:3) _____

10. "For you put up with fools gladly, since you yourselves are wise!" (2 Corinthians 11:19) _____

11. "For when I am weak, then I am strong." (2 Corinthians 12:10) _____

12. "For God is not unjust to forget your work and labor of love which you have shown toward His name" (Hebrews 6:10) _____

Problems 13–16: Identify three different figures of thought used in each of the given Bible passages. Briefly defend your answer.

13. "Where were you when I laid the foundations of the earth? Tell Me, if you have understanding. Who determined its measurements? Surely you know!" (Job 38:4–5)

_____
_____
_____
_____

Fitting Words: Workbook | EXERCISE 28A 147

14. "All flesh is grass, and all its loveliness is like the flower of the field." (Isaiah 40:6)

15. "O Ephraim, what shall I do to you? O Judah, what shall I do to you? For your faithfulness is like a morning cloud, and like the early dew it goes away." (Hosea 6:4)

16. "You are already full! You are already rich! You have reigned as kings without us—and indeed I could wish you did reign, that we also might reign with you!" (1 Corinthians 4:8)

Problems 17–20: Give the Bible reference for the verses alluded to in the given speech excerpts.

17. "I compelled to carry the gospel of freedom beyond my own home town. Like Paul, I must constantly respond to the Macedonian call for aid."—MLK, Letter from Birmingham Jail.

18. "Now the trumpet summons us again ... to bear the burden of a long twilight struggle, year in and year out, 'rejoicing in hope, patient in tribulation'—a struggle against the common enemies of man: tyranny, poverty, disease, and war itself." JFK, Inaugural Address.

19. "They know only the rules of a generation of self-seekers. They have no vision, and when there is no vision the people perish." FDR, First Inaugural Address.

20. "If they ask us here why it is we say more on the money question than we say upon the tariff question, I reply that if protection has slain its thousands the gold standard has slain its tens of thousands." William Jennings Bryan, Cross of Gold.

EXERCISE 28B

Rewrite the sentences from Exercise 28a, problems 1–12, communicating the same information, but removing as much as possible any figures of thought.

1. _____

2. _____

3. _____

4. _____

5. _____

6. _____

7. _____

8.

9.

10.

11.

12.

Problems 13–20: Rewrite or expand this sentence using a different figure of thought for each answer. Identify the figure used. Be creative!

It was very cold outside.

13.

14.

15. _____

16. _____

17. _____

18. _____

19. _____

20. _____

21. Rewrite that same sentence again, using an allusion from a song, a story, or a poem.

_____

EXERCISE 29

NAME

DATE

1. Use the backgrounds and images given in the text to memorize the first portion of Hamlet's "To be or not to be" soliloquy.

> To be, or not to be? That is the question—
> Whether 'tis nobler in the mind to suffer
> The slings and arrows of outrageous fortune,
> Or to take arms against a sea of troubles,
> And, by opposing, end them? To die, to sleep—
> No more—and by a sleep to say we end
> The heartache and the thousand natural shocks
> That flesh is heir to—'tis a consummation
> Devoutly to be wished! To die, to sleep.
> To sleep, perchance to dream—ay, there's the rub,
> For in that sleep of death what dreams may come
> When we have shuffled off this mortal coil,
> Must give us pause. There's the respect
> That makes calamity of so long life.

2. Use the backgrounds and images method to memorize this next portion of Hamlet's "To be or not to be" soliloquy:

> For who would bear the whips and scorns of time,
> Th' oppressor's wrong, the proud man's contumely
> The pangs of despised love, the law's delay,
> The insolence of office, and the spurns
> That patient merit of th' unworthy takes,
> When he himself might his quietus make
> With a bare bodkin? Who would fardels bear,
> To grunt and sweat under a weary life,
> But that the dread of something after death,
> The undiscovered country, from whose bourn
> No traveller returns, puzzles the will,
> And makes us rather bear those ills we have
> Than fly to others that we know not of?

3. Use the repetition and removal method to memorize the last portion of Hamlet's "To be or not to be" soliloquy.

>Thus conscience does make cowards of us all,
>And thus the native hue of resolution
>Is sicklied o'er with the pale cast of thought,
>And enterprise of great pitch and moment
>With this regard their currents turn awry
>And lose the name of action.

EXERCISE 30A

NAME

DATE

Problems 1–9: For each given line, identify an emotion appropriate to it, and describe what could be done in regard to the elements of delivery to convey that emotion. Also circle any words that would be particularly emphasized (no more than a few each).

1. "What have you done, that you have stolen away unknown to me, and carried away my daughters like captives taken with the sword?"—Laban, Genesis 31:26

___

2. "But now, do not therefore be grieved or angry with yourselves because you sold me here; for God sent me before you to preserve life."—Joseph, Genesis 45:5

___

155

3. "Then all this assembly shall know that the Lord does not save with sword and spear; for the battle is the Lord's, and He will give you into our hands."—David, 1 Samuel 17:47

4. "For I say to you that God is able to raise up children to Abraham from these stones."—John the Baptist, Matthew 3:9

5. "Together let us explore the stars, conquer the deserts, eradicate disease, tap the ocean depths, and encourage the arts and commerce."—John F. Kennedy, Inaugural Address

6. "You all did love him once, not without cause: / What cause withholds you then, to mourn for him?"—Mark Antony, Shakespeare's *Julius Caesar*

Fitting Words: Workbook | EXERCISE 30A   157

7. "Look, in this place ran Cassius' dagger through. / See what a rent the envious Casca made. / Through this the well-beloved Brutus stabb'd."—Mark Antony, Shakespeare's *Julius Caesar*

8. "We few, we happy few, we band of brothers."—Henry V, St. Crispin's Day speech, Shakespeare's *Henry V*

9. "We can never be satisfied as long as our children are stripped of their selfhood and robbed of their dignity by signs stating: 'For Whites only.'"—Martin Luther King Jr., "I Have a Dream"

Problems 10–14: Read the following verses. Identify the gestures that the speaker makes in each and the thoughts or feelings that their gestures are meant to convey.

10. 2 Kings 1:13

11. Matthew 12:49

12. Luke 18:13

13. Acts 14:14

14. Acts 21:40

EXERCISE 30B

NAME

DATE

Read through this introduction to Cicero's First Oration against Catiline. Describe on the lines to the right the various elements of delivery appropriate to that part of the speech. Include specific emotions and likely changes in voice, countenance, and gesture.

When, O Catiline, do you mean to cease abusing our patience? How long is that madness of yours still to mock us? When is there to be an end of that unbridled audacity of yours, swaggering about as it does now? Do not the nightly guards placed on the Palatine Hill—do not the watches posted throughout the city—does not the alarm of the people, and the union of all good men—does not the precaution taken of assembling the senate in this most defensible place—do not the looks and countenances of this venerable body here present, have any effect upon you? Do you not feel that your plans are detected? Do you not see that your conspiracy is already arrested and rendered powerless by the knowledge which everyone here

161

possesses of it? What is there that you did last night, what the night before—where is it that you were—who was there that you summoned to meet you—what design was there which was adopted by you, with which you think that any one of us is unacquainted? Shame on the age and on its principles! The senate is aware of these things; the consul sees them; and yet this man lives. Lives! aye, he comes even into the senate. He takes a part in the public deliberations; he is watching and marking down and checking off for slaughter every individual among us. And we, gallant men that we are, think that we are doing our duty to the republic if we keep out of the way of his frenzied attacks.

WORKS CITED IN EXERCISES

In addition to the works cited in the main text, which are fully documented there, the following texts are used in this workbook.

Beckmann, Petr. "Newton." *A History of Pi*. New York: St. Martin's, 1976. 134–40. Print.

Bryan, William Jennings. "A Cross of Gold." Democratic National Convention, Chicago. 9 July 1896. Speech.

Grant, George. "An Unpopular Vision." Ligonier Ministries. *Tabletalk Magazine*, 1 Feb. 2010. Web. 11 May 2016.

King, Martin Luther, Jr. "Letter from Birmingham Jail," as published in *Gospel of Freedom*, Jonathan Rieder. New York: Bloomsbury Press, 2013. Print.

Roosevelt, Franklin D. "First Inaugural Address." U. S. Capitol, Washington D.C. 4 Mar. 1933. Speech.

Shakespeare, William. "Hamlet, Prince of Denmark." Act III, Scene 1. *Shakespeare II. Great Books of the Western World*. Ed. Mortimer Adler. Second ed. Vol. 25. Chicago: Encyclopedia Britannica, 1990. 47 Print.

Wilson, Woodrow. "War Speech." U.S. Congress, Washington D.C. 2 Apr. 1917. Speech.

SPEECH JUDGING SHEETS

The judging sheets on the following pages are identical to the ones your teacher will be using to evaluate your speeches. We have provided them here so you can have a better idea of what to expect when you actually deliver your speeches and so you can use them for self-evaluation as you practice.

SPEECH JUDGING SHEET
LESSON 13: EMOTION SPEECH

Student name _____

Date _____

Title/Topic _____

Primary emotion desired _____

POINTS

1. The desired emotion was effectively produced and was appropriate to the topic. _____ / 5

2. Each element of the definition of the desired emotion was considered and applied. _____ / 5

3. Vivid language and descriptions were used to produce the desired emotion. _____ / 5

4. The speech was well arranged and unified, with introduction, body, conclusion. _____ / 5

5. The student was prepared, speaking audibly, clearly, and with good speed and expression, maintaining ethos. _____ / 5

   (Required time: 3–5 minutes)   Time _____

   Deduction for time _____

   TOTAL _____ / 25

Speech 1

SPEECH JUDGING SHEET
LESSON 14: FORENSIC SPEECH

Student name _____

Date _____

Name of accused _____ Circle one: ACCUSATION DEFENSE

Alleged wrong _____

POINTS

1. The speech was clearly aimed at accusing or defending the alleged wrongdoer. _____ / 5

2. The elements of the alleged wrong were clear: injury, voluntarily inflicted, contrary to law. _____ / 5

3. Means, opportunity, motive, and state of mind were appropriately addressed. _____ / 5

4. The speech properly followed the six parts of a discourse. _____ / 15

    a) Introduction: *hearers made receptive and attentive*

    b) Narration: *necessary background information given*

    c) Division: *issue made clear using stasis theory, proofs previewed*

    d) Proof: *persuasive arguments, focused on appropriate question of stasis*

    e) Refutation: *main objections sufficiently answered*

    f) Conclusion: *case powerfully summed up, appropriate emotional appeal*

5. The student was prepared, speaking audibly, clearly, with good speed and expression, maintaining ethos. _____ / 5

    (Required time: 5–8 minutes)   Time _____

    Deduction for time _____

    TOTAL _____ / 35

Speech 2

SPEECH JUDGING SHEET
LESSON 15: POLITICAL SPEECH

Student name _____

Date _____

Title/Topic _____

POINTS

1. The speech effectively urged the audience to do or not to do something based on expediency or harm. _____ / 5

2. The speech appealed to appropriate elements of happiness. _____ / 5

    Part(s) of happiness appealed to: _____

    _____

3. The speech appealed to appropriate elements of goodness. _____ / 5

    Good thing(s) appealed to: _____

    _____

4. The speech included the required parts of a discourse. _____ / 10

    a) Introduction: *hearers made receptive and attentive*

    b) Proof: *persuasive arguments used*

    c) Refutation: *objections sufficiently answered*

    d) Conclusion: *powerful summary, appropriate emotional appeal*

5. The student was prepared, speaking audibly, clearly, with good speed and expression, maintaining ethos _____ / 5

    (Required time: 4–6 minutes)   Time _____

    Deduction for time   _____

    TOTAL   _____ / 30

Speech 3

SPEECH JUDGING SHEET
LESSON 15: SAINT CRISPIN'S DAY

Student name _____

Date _____

What's he that wishes so?
My cousin Westmoreland? No my fair cousin:
If we are mark'd to die, we are enow
To do our country loss; and if to live,
The fewer men, the greater share of honour.
God's will! I pray thee, wish not one man more.
By Jove, I am not covetous for gold,
Nor care I who doth feed upon my cost;
It yearns me not if men my garments wear;
Such outward things dwell not in my desires;
But if it be a sin to covet honour,
I am the most offending soul alive.
No, faith, my coz, wish not a man from England:
God's peace! I would not lose so great an honour
As one man more, methinks, would share from me
For the best hope I have. O, do not wish one more!
Rather, proclaim it, Westmoreland, through my host,
That he which hath no stomach to this fight,
Let him depart; his passport shall be made
And crowns for convoy put into his purse:
We would not die in that man's company
That fears his fellowship to die with us.
This day is called the feast of Crispian:
He that outlives this day and comes safe home
Will stand a tip-toe when the day is named,
And rouse him at the name of Crispian.
He that shall live this day and see old age,
Will yearly on the vigil feast his neighbors,
And say, "Tomorrow is Saint Crispian":
Then will he strip his sleeve and show his scars,
And say, "These wounds I had on Crispin's day."
Old men forget; yet all shall be forgot,
But he'll remember with advantages
What feats he did that day: Then shall our names,
Familiar in his mouth as household words,
Harry the King, Bedford and Exeter,
Warwick and Talbot, Salisbury and Gloucester,
Be in their flowing cups freshly remember'd.
This story shall the good man teach his son;
And Crispin Crispian shall ne'er go by,
From this day to the ending of the world,
But we in it shall be remembered;
We few, we happy few, we band of brothers;
For he today that sheds his blood with me
Shall be my brother; be he ne'er so vile,
This day shall gentle his condition:
And gentlemen in England now a-bed
Shall think themselves accursed they were not here,
And hold their manhoods cheap whiles any speaks
That fought with us upon Saint Crispin's day.

CONTENT SCORING

−2 points	Lost a line
−1 point	Additional line lost, lost phrase, lines swapped
−½ point	Lost a word, phrases swapped
−⅓ point	Incorrect word, words swapped
−1 point	Restarting at a previous line
−½ point	Corrected word, major inappropriate pause
−⅓ point	Momentary inappropriate pause, repeated word
−1 point	for each word hint.

Speech 4

	POINTS LOST

CONTENT *(from front of sheet)*

    Number of hints: _____

    Other problems with content _____

VOICE

    Unclear, mumbling, not enunciating _____

    Saying *um, uh, oops…* _____

    Improper pronunciation _____

    Too fast _____

    Too quiet, could not hear easily _____

    Other problems with voice _____

                                TOTAL ____/30

SPEECH JUDGING SHEET
LESSON 16: CEREMONIAL SPEECH JUDGING

Student name _____

Date _____

Title/Topic _____

POINTS

1. The speech effectively praised someone using the appropriate methods. _____ / 15

   a) Forms of virtue: *justice, courage, temperance, magnificence, magnanimity, liberality, gentleness, prudence, wisdom, other:* _____

   b) Noble things: *courage, justice, reward is honor, good deeds, deserve to be remembered, deeds done for others, victory, not surrendering, honor, exceptional deeds, continue after death, not to practice any sordid craft, distinctive qualities, appropriate actions, finer being, quality esteemed by audience:* _____

   c) Heightening: *first one, only one, almost only one, better than others, unexpected given circumstances, same success often, observances devised to honor such achievements, compared with others, compared with famous*

2. The student showed skill in use of words (persuasive, creative). _____ / 5

3. The speech included the required parts of a discourse. _____ / 10

   a) Introduction: *hearers made receptive and attentive*

   b) Narration: *helpful background information given*

   c) Proof: *persuasive arguments used*

   d) Conclusion: *powerful summary, appropriate emotional appeal*

4. The student was prepared, speaking audibly, clearly, with good speed and expression, maintaining ethos _____ / 5

Speech 5

Speech 5

(Required time: 4–6 minutes)

Time _____

Deduction for time _____

TOTAL _____ **/ 35**

SPEECH JUDGING SHEET
FINAL SPEECH

Student name _____

Date _____

Thesis _____

POINTS

INVENTION

1. Thesis was clear, interesting, disputable but provable. All points relate to thesis. _____ / 5

2. Arguments by example were strong, enthymemes were sound. _____ / 5

3. The student demonstrated mastery of the topic, no obvious weaknesses. _____ / 5

ARRANGEMENT

4. Introduction: hearers made receptive and attentive. _____ / 5

5. Narration: terms clearly defined, necessary background information given. _____ / 5

6. Division: the issue was made clear, proofs previewed. _____ / 5

7. Proof: arguments were persuasive and properly arranged. _____ / 5

8. Refutation: all reasonable objections presented and persuasively answered. _____ / 5

9. Conclusion: case powerfully summed up, appropriate emotional appeal. _____ / 5

STYLE

10. Proper grammar and pronunciation, no obvious errors. _____ / 5

11. Speech produced the proper emotions in the hearers. _____ / 5

12. Use of figures and allusions was engaging, fitting, and made the concepts clear. _____ / 5

Speech 6

13. Level of style (simple, middle, grand) fitting to the topic and the audience. _____ / 5

MEMORY

14. The student was well prepared, made proper use of notes. _____ / 5

15. Use of eye contact kept the audience engaged. _____ / 5

DELIVERY

16. The student's appearance and dress demonstrated respect. _____ / 5

17. Good volume and enunciation, volume varied appropriately. _____ / 5

18. Voice was engaging, not monotone; student appeared interested in the topic. _____ / 5

19. Student did not speak too quickly, appropriate use of pause. _____ / 5

20. Student stood with good posture, proper facial expressions and gestures. _____ / 5

    (Required time: 8–12 minutes)   Time _____

                                               Deduction for time _____

                                               TOTAL   ___/100